Before he was president, before he changed
Ghana, before he dreamed of a united Africa...
He was just a boy. Like you.
His name is Kwame Nkrumah and this is his story.

Published by Enna's Press
ISBN: 979-8-9945-835-7-9

Library of Congress Control Number: 2026905934

Art & Design: Created using licensed assets from Canva Pro.

For more books by the author, visit : iqralittlepages.com

JUVENILE NONFICTION / Biography & Autobiography / Cultural, Ethnic & Regional
JUVENILE NONFICTION / History / Africa

Printed in USA. First Edition 2026.

Note to Parents & Educators

Dear Grown-ups,

A big dream often starts with a small but powerful thought: "*I can change something.*" For a child, discovering that they come from a line of dreamers and doers is a gift that lasts a lifetime. This book introduces your toddler to one of Africa's greatest leaders: Kwame Nkrumah - a little boy from Nkroful who grew up to dream of a united Africa.

Inside these pages, your little one will discover:

- Simple truths about unity, courage, and big dreams
- A deep love for community and homeland
- That their story is a proud part of a larger, vibrant tapestry

Our hope is that every child in Ghana, across Africa, and around the world, closes this book feeling one thing: "*I can dream big too.*"

"Forward ever, backward never." - Dr. Kwame Nkrumah

Happy reading and dreaming! Discover more books at : iqralittlepages.com

Sherifa E. Cudjoe
Author & Parent

For Mawunyo

SMALL BEGINNINGS
Kwame Nkrumah was born in Nkroful in the year 1909. A small fishing village. Every big story starts small. Your story starts here.

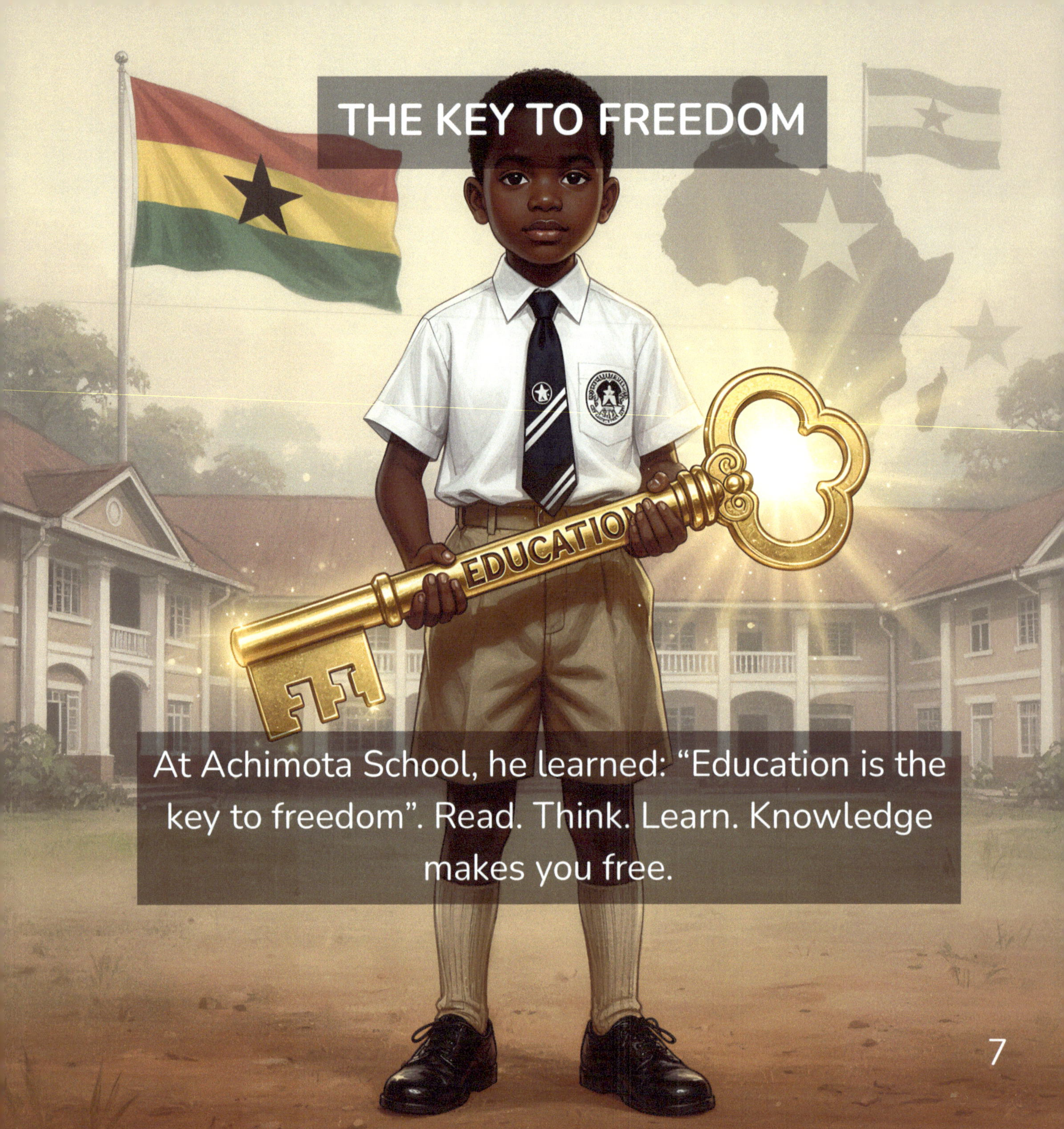

At Achimota School, he learned: "Education is the key to freedom". Read. Think. Learn. Knowledge makes you free.

TRAVELING TO LEARN

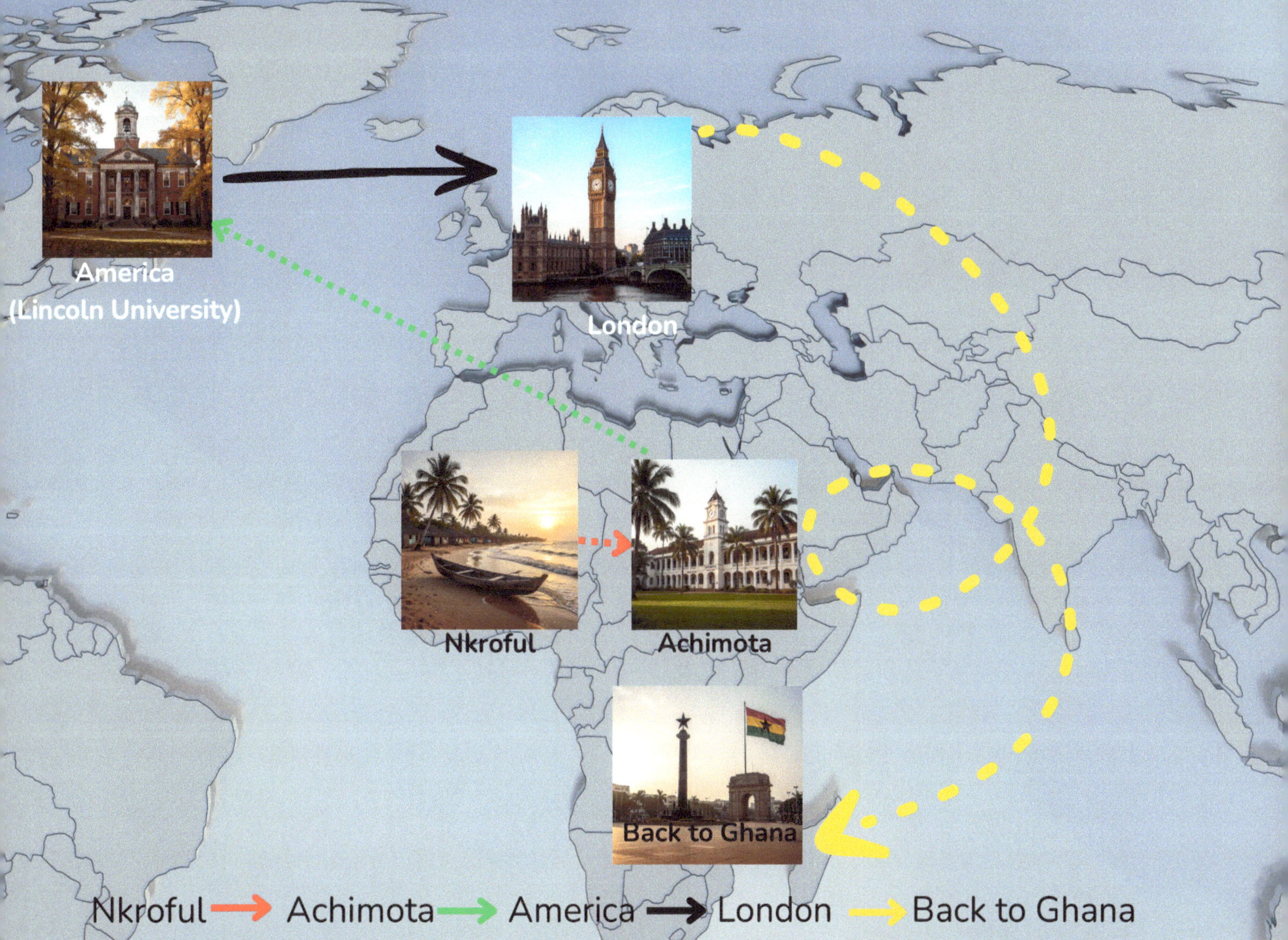

He traveled for 10 years to study. America. London. But always remembered: "I must return to free my people." Love your home

THE BIG SPEECH (1949)

In Accra, in the year 1949, he told thousands:
"We prefer self-government with danger to
servitude in tranquility."
This means: Better to lead ourselves, even if hard,
than be ruled by others, even if peaceful.
Choose your own path.

9

POSITIVE ACTION

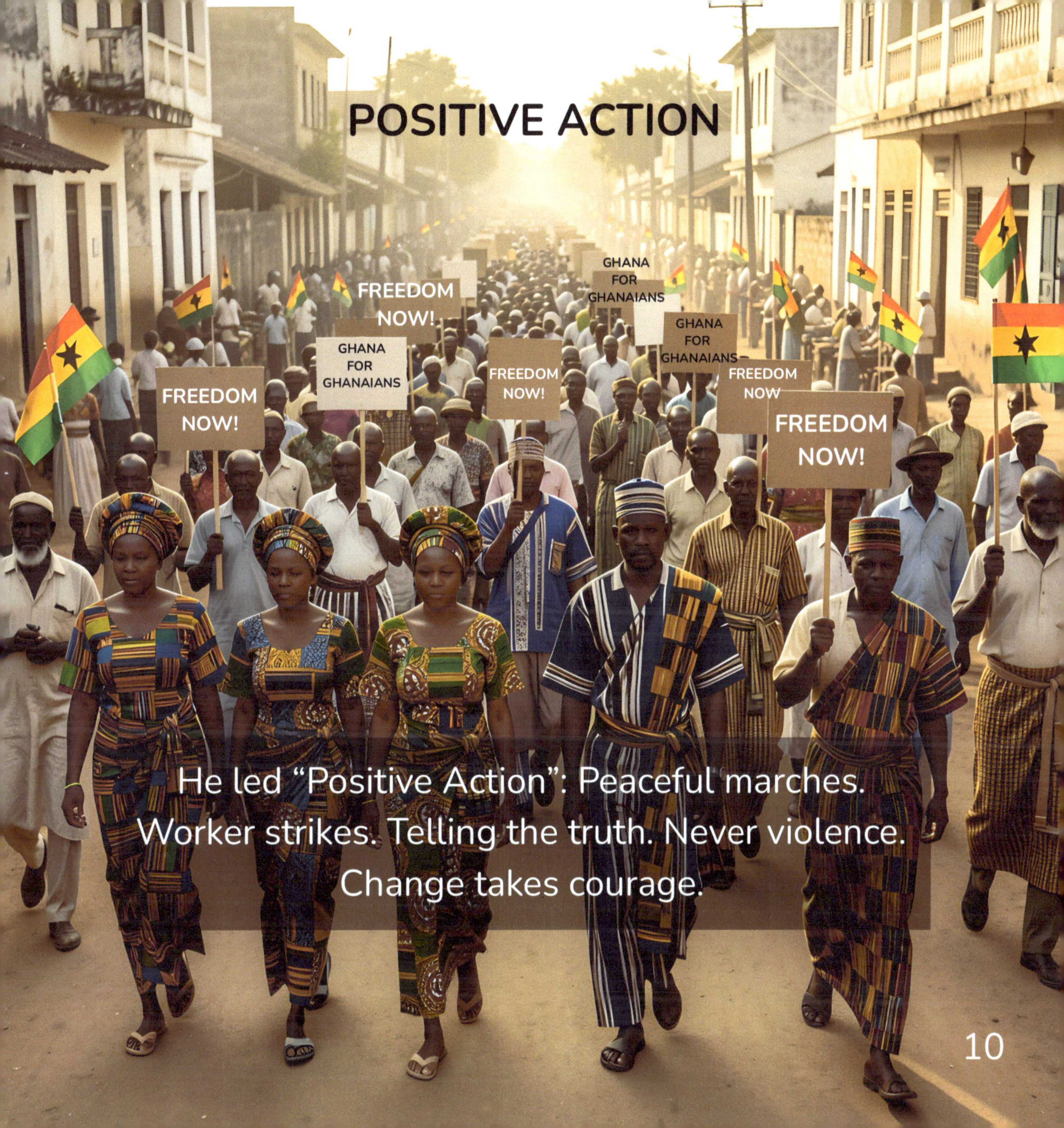

He led "Positive Action": Peaceful marches. Worker strikes. Telling the truth. Never violence. Change takes courage.

INDEPENDENCE DAY!

"At long last, the battle has ended! Ghana, your beloved country is free forever! "
His exact words that day. First African country to gain independence on March 6, 1957.
Be brave. Be first.

BUILDING GHANA

President Nkrumah built for Ghana's future: Education, Health, Power, Trade. Build what lasts for generations.

THE BLACK STAR GUIDES

The Black Star of Africa. A symbol: Ghana
would guide Africa to freedom.
By 1963, 32 African countries were free!
Be a light for others.

"Africa Must Unite!" - his famous book title. He helped create the Organization of African Unity (OAU)."Our independence is meaningless unless linked to Africa's freedom". Together we are stronger.

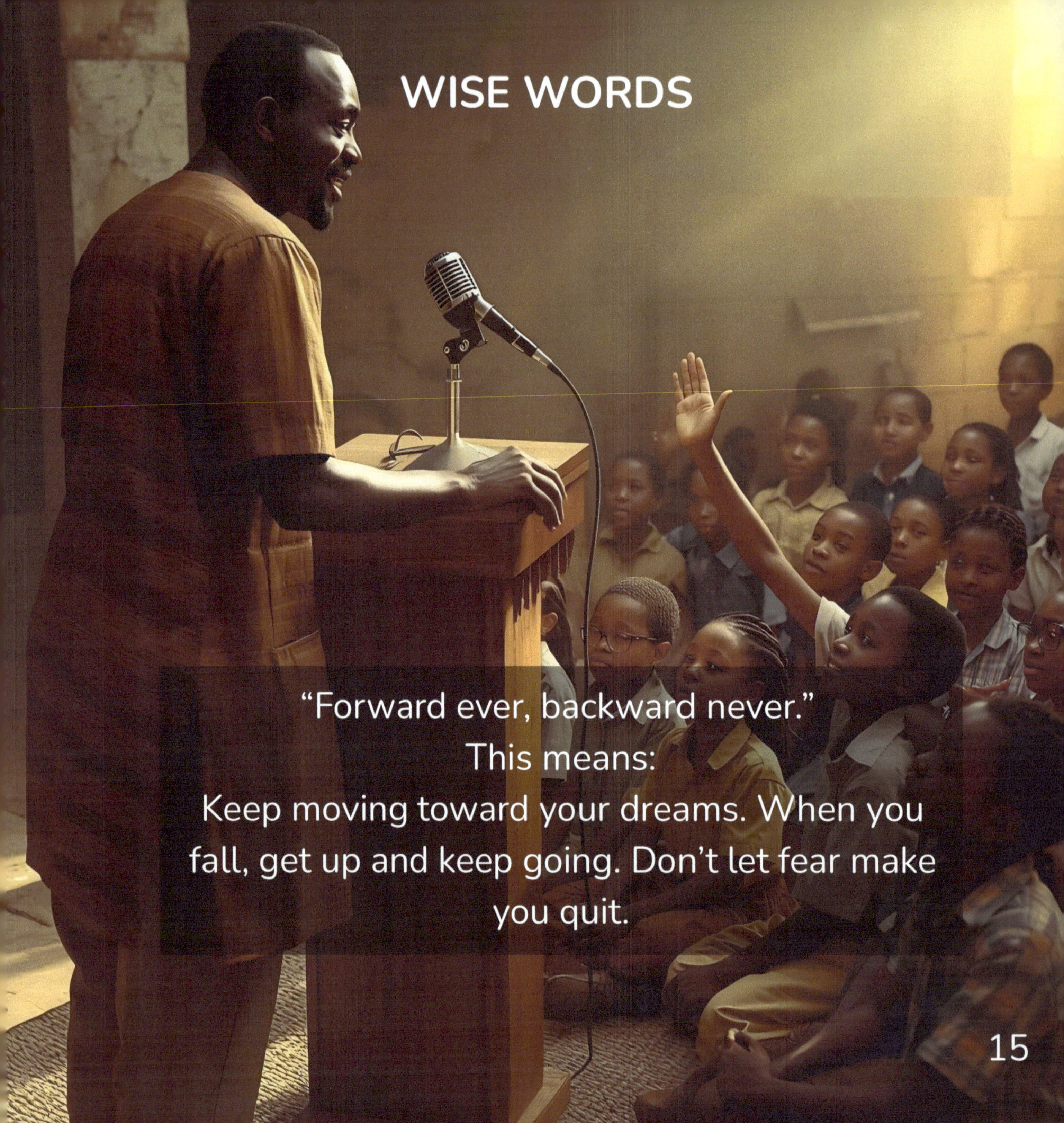

WISE WORDS

"Forward ever, backward never."
This means:
Keep moving toward your dreams. When you fall, get up and keep going. Don't let fear make you quit.

15

WISE WORDS

"We face neither East nor West. We face forward."
This means:
We don't copy others blindly. We think for ourselves. We choose our own Ghanaian way.
Always ask: "What is right?" Not "What does everyone else do?"
Simple truth: Believe in yourself.

THE STORM

Not everyone agreed with his speed. Some feared change. In the year 1966, while Nkrumah was in China, soldiers took over. He never returned to Ghana. But ideas cannot be arrested.

HIS LIGHT SHINES
Today, because Kwame Nkrumah believed:
• Ghana governs Ghana
• Political freedom is just the beginning
• Education is your right
His light still shines. Protect your freedom.
18

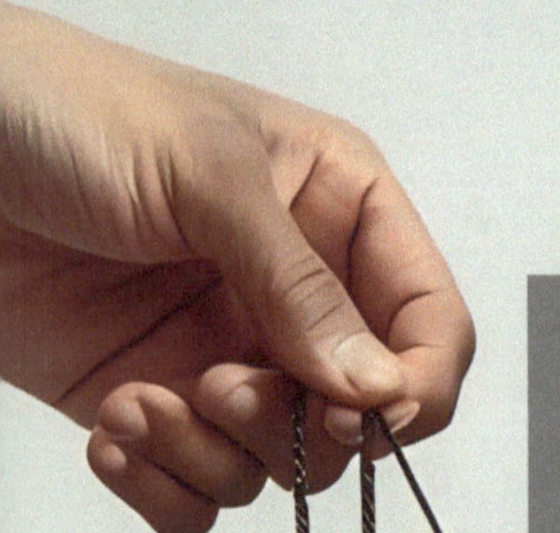

NKRUMAH'S WARNING : NEO-COLONIALISM

Nkrumah saw this coming.
He warned that foreign money would be used "for the exploitation rather than for the development" of Africa.
Some African countries are still fighting for true economic freedom. The struggle continues.
That's why WE must stay awake. That's why WE must learn.
That's why WE must lead.

YOUR TURN TO LEAD

Kwame Nkrumah was once a child like you.
He asked questions.
He dreamed.
Now it's YOUR turn.

MY POSITIVE ACTION PLAN

Montessori Practical Life Task:

1. **Red Strip:** "What problem do I see?" (Child draws/describes)

2. **Gold Strip:** "What can I build/do?" (Their solution)

3. **Green Strip:** "Who will this help?" (Community focus)

4. **Black Star:** "My name as a problem-solver"